Life in Tudor Times

Brian Williams

Raintree

Contents

Some words are shown in **bold**, like this. You can find out what they mean by looking in the glossary.

Introducing the Tudors

The first Tudor king of England was Henry VII. He ruled from 1485 to 1509. The last of the Tudors was Queen Elizabeth I, who ruled from 1558 to 1603.

A Tudor king or queen could do much as they liked – build a palace, order an execution, even start a war. They had **ministers** to give them advice, and a **Parliament**, but Parliament had much less power than today. Rich lords at **Court** could do much as they liked, too (except annoy the king or queen). Powerful men ran the Christian Church. Ordinary people – **merchants**, farmers, and poor people – had little say in how they were ruled.

◀ This is a portrait of Henry VIII, painted in about 1540 by his court painter Hans Holbein.

Portraits show us what people looked like. Painters often made important people look powerful with rich clothes and jewels.

www.raintreepublishers.co.uk
Visit our website to find out more information about Raintree books.

To order:
☎ Phone 0845 6044371
🖷 Fax +44 (0) 1865 312263
🖳 Email myorders@raintreepublishers.co.uk

Customers from outside the UK please telephone +44 1865 312262

Raintree is an imprint of Capstone Global Library Limited, a company incorporated in England and Wales having its registered office at 7 Pilgrim Street, London, EC4V 6LB - Registered company number: 6695582

Text © Capstone Global Library Limited 2010
First published in hardback in 2010
First published in paperback in 2011
The moral rights of the proprietor have been asserted.

Edited by Kate de Villiers and Laura Knowles
Designed by Steve Mead and Debbie Oatley
Original illustrations © Capstone Global Library Limited 2010
Illustrations by Linden Artists – Steve Weston (p. 12) and
    Adam Hook (pp. 19 and 24)
Picture research by Mica Brancic and Elaine Willis
Production by Alison Parsons
Originated by Chroma Graphics (Overseas) Pte. Ltd
Printed and bound in China by Leo Paper Products Ltd

ISBN 978 0 431193 61 8 (hardback)
14 13 12 11 10
10 9 8 7 6 5 4 3 2 1

ISBN 978 0 431193 68 7 (paperback)
15 14 13 12 11
10 9 8 7 6 5 4 3

British Library Cataloguing in Publication Data
Williams, Brian, 1943-
Life in Tudor times. -- (Unlocking history)
942'.05-dc22
A full catalogue record for this book is available from the British Library.

Acknowledgements
We would like to thank the following for permission to reproduce photographs: We would like to thank the following for permission to reproduce photographs: Alamy pp. **6** (© The London Art Archive), **10** (John Glover), **23** (© John Joannides); Corbis p. **11** (Robert Harding World Imagery/© John Miller); The Art Archive pp. **16**, **22** (Eileen Tweedy/Magdalene College Cambridge); The Bridgeman Art Library pp. **4** (© Philip Mould Ltd, London/Private Collection), **8** (© British Library Board. All Rights Reserved/British Library, London, UK), **14** (Rafael Valls Gallery, London, UK), **17** (Private Collection), **18** (National Maritime Museum, London, UK), **20** (The Crown Estate), **27** (Giraudon/Lauros/Service Historique de la Marine, Vincennes, France); TopFoto p. **13** (HIP/The Print Collector).

Cover photograph of William Brooke, 10th Lord Cobham and his family, 1567, by Master of the Countess of Warwick (fl. 1567–69) reproduced with permission of Bridgeman Art Library/Longleat House, Wiltshire, UK.

We would like to thank Bill Marriott for his invaluable help in the preparation of this book.

Henry VIII was king of England from 1509 until 1547. He had six wives. Henry's three children ruled after him, in turn. They were Edward VI, Mary I, and Elizabeth I. Elizabeth gave her name to the "Elizabethan age". It was a time of change. There were wars, plots, new ideas, and **voyages** to strange lands. It was exciting to be a Tudor, but dangerous, too.

This book shows how we can unlock history, using **evidence** from all kinds of sources. The yellow key boxes explain how different sources tell us about life in Tudor times.

A family tree shows a person's relatives from the past to the present.

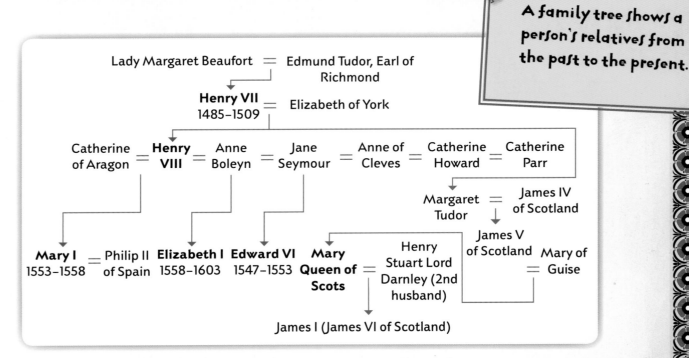

This is the Tudor family tree. Elizabeth I had no children. When she died in 1603, her nearest **heir**, James VI of Scotland, became King James I of England.

"She is much attached to the people," said the Spanish ambassador in 1558, when Elizabeth I became queen.

Quotations like the one above show what people at the time thought.

Rival kingdoms

In the 1500s, England and Scotland were separate countries. They were not always friendly. The English fought the Scots in 1513 and again in 1542. England also fought France and Spain.

England and Scotland were small countries. Europe's strongest country was Spain. Spain ruled parts of Holland, Italy, and Germany. Spain also had an **empire** in America, after conquering the Aztecs of Mexico and the Incas of Peru.

▼ In 1520, Henry VIII and the king of France held a grand meeting. This painting shows Henry's ships setting sail for France.

Tudor England grew stronger and its navy challenged the might of Spain. English ships attacked Spanish America. Queen Elizabeth I tried to keep peace with Spain. One way she did this was to keep everyone guessing about which European prince or king she might marry. In the end, she married no-one.

Spain and England also quarrelled about religion. Most people in Europe were Christians, but they were divided. People were either **Catholics**, obeying the **Pope** in Rome, or **Protestants** wanting to make their own rules. Spain was Catholic. England was mainly Protestant. Both Catholics and Protestants were ready to die for their beliefs.

Mary Queen of Scots
Mary Queen of Scots (1542–87) was queen of Scotland by birth, queen of France by marriage, and might have become a Catholic queen of England. She was next in line, after Elizabeth. In 1567, Mary was forced to leave Scotland for England, where she was kept a prisoner and was finally executed for plotting against Elizabeth. Her son James became king of Scotland and England.

▼ This block chart compares the biggest empires in Tudor times.

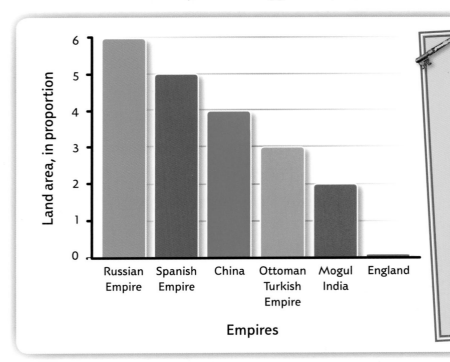

The blocks in this chart help us compare the size of different empires. It shows that the Russian Empire's land area was about twice as big as the Ottoman Turkish Empire, and that England's land area was very small compared to the great empires of the world.

Town and country

London was Tudor England's only big city. By 1600, London had 200,000 people. The next biggest city was Norwich, with about 15,000 people. London was the centre of government, with palaces, theatres, churches, and narrow streets crammed with houses and workshops. London was also a busy port for **trade**.

Only one in ten Tudors lived in a town. Most people lived in the countryside. Some owned farms. Poor people worked for rich farmers. Sheep's wool was England's most important export (goods that were sold to another country).

Most families had at least four children. Rich families needed sons to take over their land. They hoped for more than one boy, because many babies died of diseases. The first few years of life were the most dangerous.

▲ This Tudor painting shows people shearing sheep (clipping off the wool). It also shows what people's clothes and houses looked like.

Fun fact

Tudor England had three sheep for every one person!

Fast-growing London

In Tudor times, the number of people living in London grew quickly, as this graph shows. Coventry counted its **citizens** in 1586 — there were 6,502 people. London's population was more than 10 times bigger. England had no **census**. Most population figures are based on tax and church records.

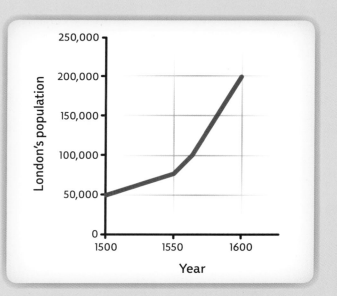

In 1598, historian John Stow complained about London's traffic. He thought there were too many carts and coaches, and that "the streets and lanes are so narrow as to make this dangerous".

Tudor writers such as Stow tell us about everyday life. Stow tells us how busy London was getting, and what people like him thought about it.

Tudor Money

This chart outlines the yearly amount of money earned by people in different jobs or positions. It shows the wide gap between the very rich and the very poor. Tudor money was in pounds, shillings, and pence (written as £1 1s 1d). It is not easy to compare prices with today's.

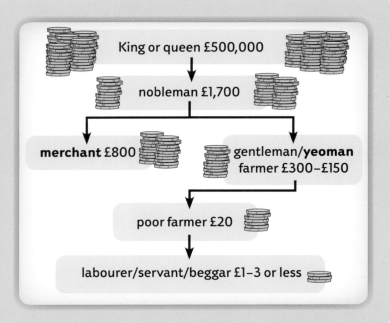

Home life

A few Tudor houses are still standing. Evidence for others comes from pictures – and bills! In 1505, a builder called Thomas Binks was paid £8 8s 8d (£8.43) for "the gallery and orchard" at Henry VII's palace at Richmond. More evidence comes from wills (see page 11) and **inventories** (see page 13).

Rich Tudors spent a lot of money on their homes and gardens. Builders' bills show us what kinds of "home improvements" were done in Tudor times.

Rich people lived in large houses. Some had castles, though by Tudor times castles were out-of-date. Rich **merchants** built new houses of brick with fireplaces and chimneys. Big houses had lots of rooms, including a great hall, bedrooms, a parlour for family meals, storerooms, a kitchen, and gardens.

▼ This is a Tudor "knot garden". Herbs, hedges, and bushes were planted and trimmed to make shapes and patterns.

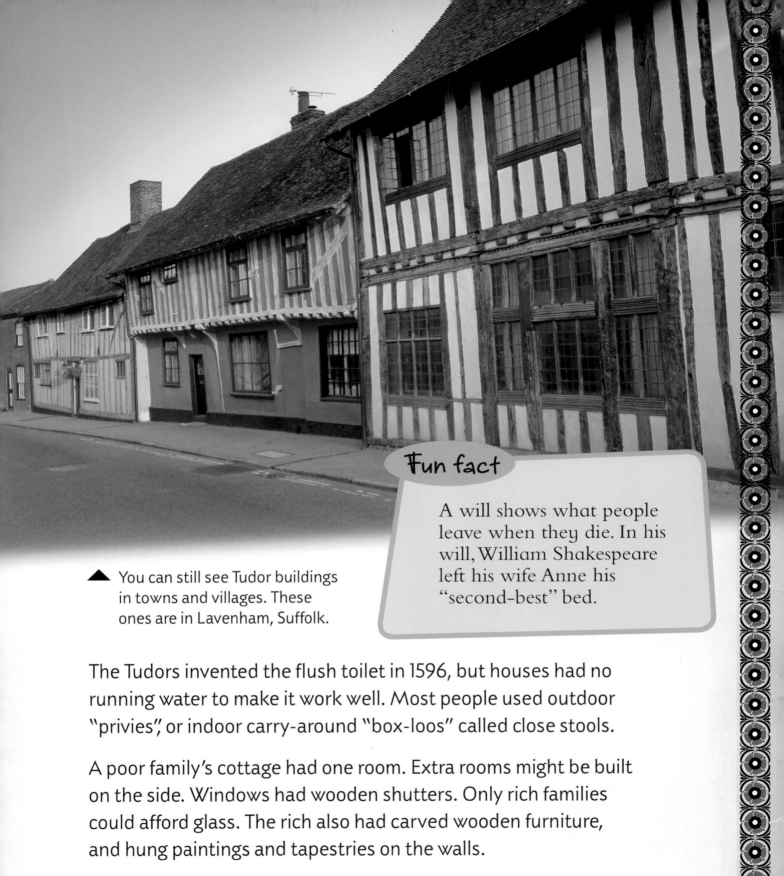

▲ You can still see Tudor buildings in towns and villages. These ones are in Lavenham, Suffolk.

Fun fact

A will shows what people leave when they die. In his will, William Shakespeare left his wife Anne his "second-best" bed.

The Tudors invented the flush toilet in 1596, but houses had no running water to make it work well. Most people used outdoor "privies", or indoor carry-around "box-loos" called close stools.

A poor family's cottage had one room. Extra rooms might be built on the side. Windows had wooden shutters. Only rich families could afford glass. The rich also had carved wooden furniture, and hung paintings and tapestries on the walls.

In London, houses were squashed together, with upper storeys sticking out. People could lean out of a window and shake hands with neighbours across the street.

Clothes

Rich people spent lots of money on clothes. William Harrison wrote crossly in 1577: "How much cost is bestowed nowadays upon our bodies, and how little upon our souls?"

Rich men's clothes were padded, stiffened, or slashed. Men wore ruffs (fancy collars) and earrings, and were fussy about haircuts and beards. Rich women wore a hooped under-skirt, or farthingale, sometimes padded around the hips so the skirt stuck out on either side. Outdoors, people wore cloaks and hats. In winter, big houses were cold. Tudor pictures show people wearing warm robes and furs. Men and women used perfumes, to cover up the stink in homes and streets.

▲ This picture shows a rich man and woman. What Tudors wore showed how rich they were. The finer the clothes and jewels, the richer the wearer.

Poor people made their own clothes. Women wore long dresses. Men wore a shirt, short trousers or breeches, stockings, and a jerkin (jacket of leather). Children often ran barefoot. Babies were tightly wrapped in bands of cloth, to keep their arms and legs straight.

Poor people, like these peasants, wore simple clothes for the day's work.

Fun fact

Wash-day thieves

On wash-day, people hung clothes to dry on hedges. Thieves called "prigmen" used sticks to steal drying clothes! We learn this from a 1575 book *The Fraternity of Vagabonds* by John Awdeley, all about Tudor thieves and tricksters.

Books such as Awdeley's, written at the time, tell us about Tudor "low life".

A peek into the wardrobe

An **inventory** of London **merchant** William Powncett's wardrobe lists:

"A worsted (woollen) gown lined with black lamb ... an old coat of black velvet ... a satin night cap, a pair of new gloves, and a gown lined with squirrel skins ..."

This inventory was made when he died in 1553 and is kept in the Essex Record Office. It shows that he was a rich man, but kept his old warm clothes, too.

Food and drink

The poor ate a kind of stew called potage, porridge, bread, and vegetables. Meat was a treat. Rich people ate much more, even in prison! When the Duchess of Somerset was shut up in the Tower of London in 1552, she was served meat every day for dinner. For supper one day she was served 12 larks (small birds). At a feast, guests might dine on swan, peacock, sturgeon (a huge fish), venison (deer), and beef, followed by fruit pies, cakes, puddings, custards, and jellies. A rich host showed off by offering lots of fine foods and drink to guests – especially if Queen Elizabeth I came to visit!

People drank milk, water, wine, and a drink called ale, made by brewing grain. Many people brewed ale at home, and baked their own bread. Potatoes, tomatoes, tea, and chocolate first came to Britain in Tudor times, but before 1600 few people had tasted these new foods.

▼ This painting shows a well-dressed family saying grace (a prayer of thanks) before enjoying a meal.

A Tudor cookery book, *The Good Housewives Treasury* (1588), has a tasty recipe for pippen pie (apple pie) with cinnamon, orange peel, and sugar. Liking too much sugar, and not brushing their teeth properly, meant many people had bad teeth. Elizabeth I's teeth turned black! A recipe for eel pie tells cooks to add sugar and pears to the fish, which sounds strange to us.

Meal times

In his book *Description of England* (1577), William Harrison tells us that rich people ate dinner around noon (12 p.m.) and supper between 5 and 6 p.m. "The poorest sort (poor people) generally dine and sup when they may …". Most poor people worked from sunrise to sunset, and so ate their meals whenever they could take a break.

Lady Margaret Hoby kept a diary from the 1590s. She tells of a visit to her friend Lady Walsingham:
"after I came home I was pained with the toothache, which continued with me four days …"

A diary can contain fascinating information about a person's daily life, including weather, pets, friends – and toothache!

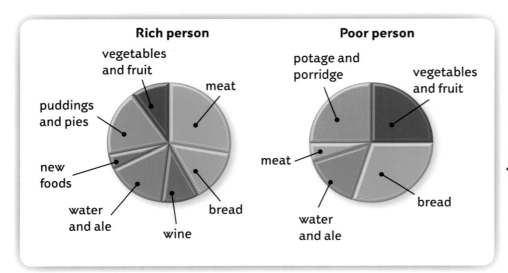

Rich person

vegetables and fruit
meat
puddings and pies
new foods
water and ale
wine
bread

Poor person

potage and porridge
vegetables and fruit
meat
water and ale
bread

◀ These pie charts compare foods that rich and poor people would have eaten.

Going to school

Poor children worked as soon as they were big enough to watch sheep or scare crows. Farm boys learned to plough (with oxen and horses). Girls learned to milk cows, and make butter and cheese.

Girls did not go to school. Girls in rich families had home teachers. However, most boys, including some poor boys, did go to school. Lessons included Latin and English, not much science or maths, but plenty of reading from the Bible. Poor boys went to school part-time, so they could work the rest of the day. "Every child of six or seven learns a trade," wrote Thomas Wilson in his book *The State of England* (1600). Many boys worked as **apprentices**.

▼ This picture, made in about 1560, shows a Tudor school. What does it tell us about what schools were like?

Fun fact

Tudor football was rougher than modern rugby or football. The writer Sir Thomas Elyot said the game was "nothing but beastly fury and extreme violence".

Games in Tudor times included skittles or nine-pins, bowls, and "crickett". Children played with bats and balls, hoops, and kites. They swam, climbed trees, and in winter went ice skating. Dolls with jointed legs and arms, or model ships, were expensive, so poor children had home-made toys.

In 1589, a schoolboy wrote in his Latin book: "John Slye is my name, And with my pen I write the same, God that made both sea and land, Give me grace to mend [improve] my hand. The rose is red, the leaves are green, God save Elizabeth, our noble Queen."

A princess with talent

Elizabeth I (1533–1603) was the daughter of Henry VIII's second wife, Anne Boleyn (who had her head chopped off in 1536). The young princess Elizabeth was taught at home. She learned French, Italian, and Latin and loved horse riding.

Tudors did not worry too much about spelling. John Slye probably also wrote his name "Slie" or "Sly". His verse, written the year after England's fight with the Spanish Armada, shows that he was religious and felt proud to be English.

Rich Tudors enjoyed "hawking" – hunting with trained hawks and falcons.

Explorers

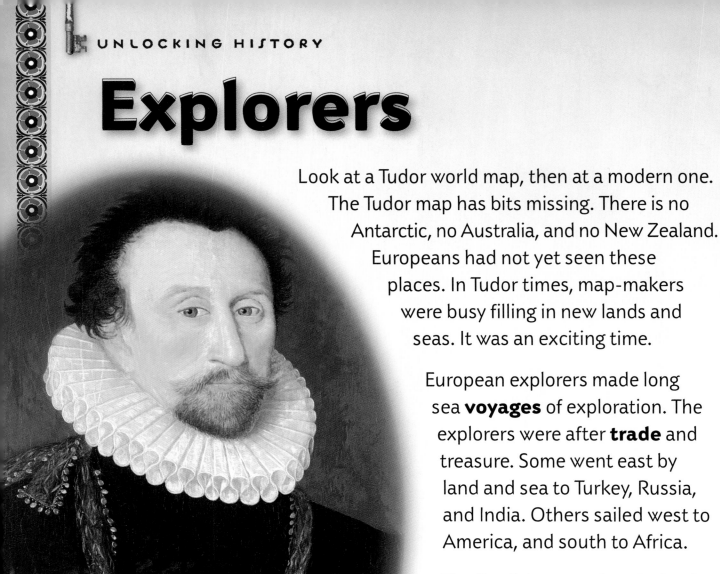

Look at a Tudor world map, then at a modern one. The Tudor map has bits missing. There is no Antarctic, no Australia, and no New Zealand. Europeans had not yet seen these places. In Tudor times, map-makers were busy filling in new lands and seas. It was an exciting time.

European explorers made long sea **voyages** of exploration. The explorers were after **trade** and treasure. Some went east by land and sea to Turkey, Russia, and India. Others sailed west to America, and south to Africa.

The English started exploring in the 1490s. At first, they steered clear of lands controlled by Spain and Portugal. In the 1560s, Sir John Hawkins began trading African **slaves** to America. English ships began trading, but also made bold attacks to steal Spanish silver and gold. These pirate raids were supposedly unofficial, but Queen Elizabeth I knew of them. One of the biggest prizes was the capture of the Portuguese ship *Madre de Dios* in 1592.

▲ This is a portrait of the sea captain Sir John Hawkins. He was born in 1532 and died while on an expedition to the Caribbean in 1595.

Timeline of important English voyages

1497	John Cabot sails to Canada
1508	Sebastian Cabot sails to Canada
1527	John Rut sails to Canada and Florida
1553	Richard Chancellor goes by sea and land to Russia
1562	John Hawkins sails to Africa
1576	Martin Frobisher sails to Canada
1577–80	Francis Drake sails around the world

Timelines show when and where things happened.

The Tudors and Africa

Europeans bought slaves in Africa with guns, cloth, and rum. The slaves were sold in America for sugar and gold. Some Africans arrived in England. By the 1590s, church records show there were black people living in London.

1 Spanish galleon 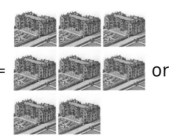 = **8 Tudor palaces**  or **28 small ships**  or **3 armies**

The Madre de Dios carried over 508 tonnes of treasure worth (in Tudor money) over £140,000. This diagram shows what you could buy with this amount of money in Tudor times. The Queen took her share too!

▲ A successful voyage could make a captain very rich. One Spanish treasure ship could be worth a fortune.

Over the oceans

Tudor seamen never knew how long a **voyage** might last. Sailing ships were blown by the wind, or left without wind for days. The first explorers did not know how big the Atlantic Ocean was (it took at least three weeks to sail across). The Pacific Ocean, first crossed by the Portuguese explorer Magellan in 1520, was twice as big!

Navigation, or finding the way, was a problem. Close to home, sailors looked for coastal landmarks such as cliffs. They worked out how far they had sailed in a day, using a sand-glass timer and a knotted rope let down into the water. They noted the position of the stars and sun, using an astrolabe. They had compasses, maps called charts, and "rutters", which were guidebooks with notes made by other sailors about dangers such as sandbanks or rocks.

Sir Francis Drake (1540–96)

Francis Drake (left) went to sea as a boy. He captained the first English ships to sail around the world, between 1577 and 1580. On his return he was made a **knight** by Queen Elizabeth I. In 1586, he brought potatoes and tobacco from Virginia in America to England. Drake died in the Caribbean on yet another raiding voyage.

Captain Martin Frobisher tried to find the Northwest Passage to Asia through the Arctic. Some ships got trapped in the ice and the sailors had to fight to save the ship from being crushed. This is how writer Richard Hakluyt (1552–1616) described Frobisher's men battling the Arctic ice:

"Having poles, pikes [spear-like weapons], pieces of timber and oars in their hands [the men] stood almost day and night without rest, bearing off the force and breaking the sway of the ice ..."

The Tudors and Africa

The Tudors thought that exploring the world was important, but there were also many dangers. Do you think it would have been a good idea to go on a voyage in Tudor times?

Reasons for going:	Dangers:
See new lands	Get lost and never be seen again
See new animals and plants	Ship sinks
Eat new foods	Die of disease
Meet new people	Die from lack of food and water
Trade and get rich	Get eaten by a sea monster
Find treasure and get even richer	Get killed by enemies

Tables are a good way to compare two sides of a question.

Tudor ships

The *Mary Rose* was a 711-tonne warship that was part of Henry VIII's navy. It sank off Portsmouth in 1545, but in 1982 archaeologists raised it. An archaeologist is someone who studies historical **evidence**, such as old objects, buildings, and other remains often found in the ground or under the sea. As well as the wooden ship and its guns, they also brought up everyday things, such as razors, fishing gear, dominoes, and even pea pods.

Mary Rose was a big ship for its time. When it sank, there were probably at least 500 people on board. It carried 15 brass guns, and more than 200 bows (fired by soldiers on board). Drake's *Golden Hind*, at only 100–150 tonnes, was much smaller than *Mary Rose*, and tiny compared with a modern cruise ship that weighs 300 times as much.

▼ A picture of the warship *Mary Rose*, from a list of King Henry VIII's ships.

A modern copy of Drake's *Golden Hind*, now docked in London.

> Building a life-size replica (copy) of a Tudor ship shows how the original was built and sailed.

The Golden Hind – some facts and figures

Length: less than 40 m (120 ft)
Masts: three
Sails: six (five square, and one lateen- or triangle-shaped)
Speed: 8 knots (15 km/h)
Guns: 22 cannons
Crew: about 110 sailors

> Statistics (facts and figures) give us details about what ships were like in Tudor times.

In 1588, King Philip of Spain planned to invade England, using an Armada (battle fleet) of 130 ships and 30,000 men. The English had 197 ships, and 16,000 men. Both sides fought bravely, but the English had the best of the sea-fights. Their ships sailed fast. The English liked to fight at long-range, with guns, and not get into hand-to-hand fights on deck. After two weeks, storms scattered the Armada and many Spanish ships were wrecked. Only 61 ships made it back to Spain.

Life at sea

Tudor seamen were tough. They braved stormy seas, snow and ice, and blistering hot sun. They climbed the rigging (ropes) to the top of the masts in all weathers. They ate rotten food, and usually slept on the deck. In the 1590s, sleeping hammocks were used for the first time. A hammock was a cloth bed, hung from each end by ropes.

▼ This is a modern illustration of a Tudor captain and a sailor, based on **evidence** from history.

captain

sailor

The captain was in command, but the most experienced seaman was usually the master. Other important jobs were master gunner, quartermaster (in charge of stores), and boatswain (known as the "bosun", he told the sailors what to do). A ship also had a surgeon, pilot, master's mate, carpenter, sail-maker, and cook. Ships' boys did odd jobs and acted as servants. There was usually a ship's cat as well.

What sailors ate

Lists show what stores and provisions (food) sailors took. For his round-the-world voyage, Drake took ale, wine, vinegar, salt, cheese, butter, oatmeal, rice, dried peas, biscuit, fish, beef, and pork (meat was salted, smoked, or dried to preserve it).

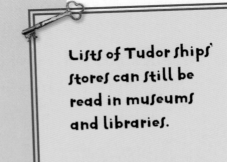

Lists of Tudor ships' stores can still be read in museums and libraries.

If a seaman did not obey orders, he was punished. He might be flogged (whipped) or put in irons (chains). Passengers were often rich young men seeking adventure.

The ship carried live chickens, goats, and pigs but most food soon went bad. Drinking water became green and slimy, so sailors prayed for rain to refill the water barrels. Fish and seabirds made a welcome change from mouldy food.

With no fresh vegetables and fruit, many men became ill with scurvy. Scurvy is a disease caused by not eating enough fresh fruit and vegetables. The men's skin turned spotty and their teeth fell out. Often, half the crew died on a long **voyage**.

First colonies

On their travels, Tudor explorers met new people – Native Americans, Africans, Polynesians, Chinese, Japanese, and Indians. They **traded** with the people they met, and learned new ways of doing things. They also brought some new foods back to England.

After 1500, people knew the world was much bigger than anyone had guessed. America was a "New World". Sir Walter Raleigh decided America was a good place to start a colony. A colony is a settlement made by one group of people in a new land. In 1585, Raleigh sent ships to Roanoke, Virginia. One of the colonists was John White, who made maps and painted what he saw. These maps and paintings are first-hand **evidence** for what life was like for Native Americans and colonists.

This first colony failed. There was not enough food, and the settlers sailed back to England. In 1587, a second colony in Roanoke also failed. This time, all the settlers mysteriously disappeared. In 1607, the English started a new colony at Jamestown. About 170 years later, Virginia was one of the first states to become part of the United States of America.

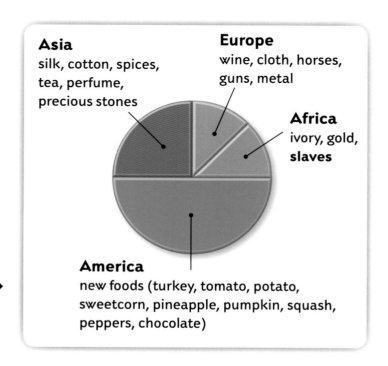

Asia
silk, cotton, spices, tea, perfume, precious stones

Europe
wine, cloth, horses, guns, metal

Africa
ivory, gold, **slaves**

America
new foods (turkey, tomato, potato, sweetcorn, pineapple, pumpkin, squash, peppers, chocolate)

This pie chart shows some of the trade goods carried in Tudor ships from around the world.

The "Lost Colony" of Roanoke had 117 people, who landed in 1587 (a baby, John White's grand-daughter, was born soon afterwards). When White sailed back to America in 1590, no-one was left. The only clues were carved on trees: the letters "CRO" and the word "Croatoan". It is possible that the colonists went to live with the friendly Croatoan Indians.

▼ This picture of Native Americans barbecuing fish was made in 1590, based on a painting by the explorer John White.

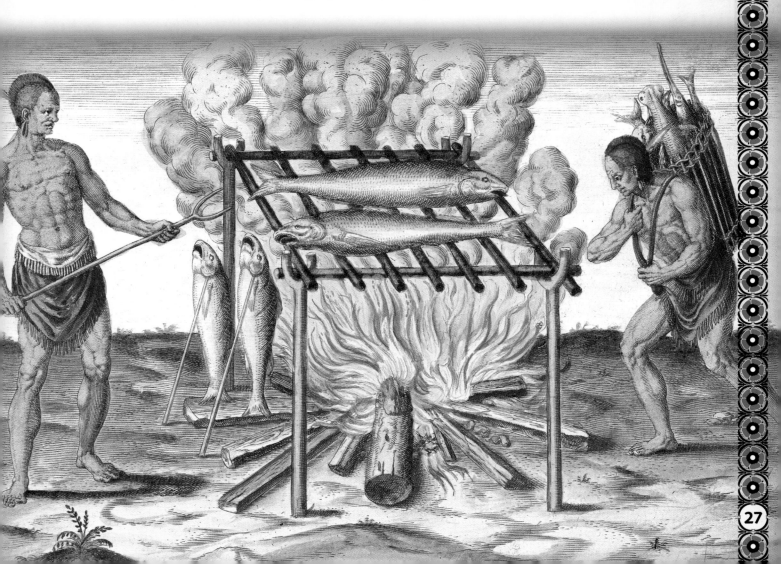

Times of change

Tudor people looked across the oceans for **trade**, treasure, and new places to live. Writers praised this new spirit of adventure. The "New World" was a good subject for writers, too. William Shakespeare's play *The Tempest* starts with a shipwreck on a lonely island. England before 1500 was a land of **knights** and castles; by 1600 ships and **merchants** had become far more important. It was the start of the British **Empire**.

Different types of **evidence**, including pictures and **quotations**, help us to unlock history and show how Britain was changing. During Tudor times, the population was growing and towns were getting busier. The way people spoke changed, as a national form of English became widely used. People tried new foods, such as potatoes, and even strange (and unhealthy) habits, such as smoking tobacco leaves in pipes.

Tudor times were not peaceful. There were several plots to kill Queen Elizabeth I, followed by the arrest and torture of the plotters, and horrible executions were common. **Protestants** and **Catholics** were burned to death for refusing to give up their faiths. It was a violent age. Yet for many people, life got better, and it was seldom dull.

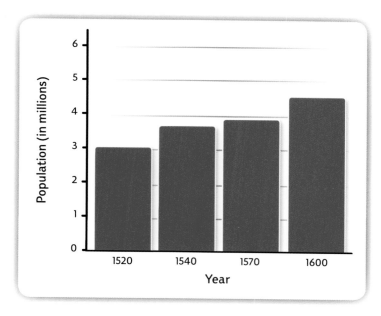

▲ This graph shows how Britain's population grew between 1520 and 1600. Today, more than 60 million people live in Britain.

Timeline

1485	Henry VII becomes the first Tudor king of England and Wales
1492	Christopher Columbus sails from Spain to America
1497–99	Vasco da Gama (Portugal) sails to India
1498	John Cabot dies seeking the Northwest Passage to Asia
1509	Henry VII dies; his son Henry VIII becomes king
1519–22	One ship of Ferdinand Magellan's expedition completes the first round-the-world voyage
1543	Polish scientist Copernicus says Earth moves around the Sun
1545	The warship *Mary Rose* sinks in the River Solent
1547	Henry VIII dies; his son Edward VI becomes king
1553	Edward VI dies; shortly after, his sister Mary I becomes queen
1558	Mary I dies; her sister Elizabeth I becomes queen
1560s	John Hawkins **trades slaves** between Africa and America
1570s	Martin Frobisher makes three voyages to Canada
1580	Francis Drake returns from his round-the-world voyage
1585	Sir Walter Raleigh starts a colony in Roanoke, America
1587	Mary Queen of Scots is executed; second Roanoke colony is begun
1588	The Spanish Armada is defeated
1590	Roanoke colony fails
1595	Sir Walter Raleigh explores in South America
1599	The Globe theatre opens in London
1600	The East India Company is set up for trade with Asia
1603	Queen Elizabeth I dies; James VI of Scotland becomes King James I of England

Glossary

apprentice young person learning a trade such as carpentry

Catholic Christian belonging to the Roman Catholic Church

census official count of a country's or city's people

citizen person who belongs to a city or state

Court rich, important people, including lords and ladies, close to the king and queen

empire large area with many peoples living under the rule of one strong country

evidence picture, writing, an object, or someone's account, which tells us how things were at a particular time

heir person who becomes king or queen after their relative dies

inventory list of a person's possessions

knight someone given the title "Sir" by the king or queen

merchant person who does business through trade

minister person who helps to run the government of a country

Parliament group of people elected or chosen to make laws on taxes and other matters

Pope head of the Catholic Church in Rome

Protestant Christian belonging to one of the churches that broke away from the Roman Catholic Church during the Reformation of the 1500s

quotation what someone says, written down

slave servant who was not free, and who belonged to a master

trade buying and selling goods

voyage sea journey by ship

yeoman farmer who was richer than a labourer but poorer than a lord

Find out more

Books

History from Buildings: Tudor Britain, Stewart Ross (Franklin Watts, 2006)
Rich and Poor in Tudor Times, Peter D. Riley (Evans Brothers Ltd, 2006)
Shakespeare's World: Daily Life, Kathy Elgin (Cherrytree Books, 2008)
Tudor Exploration, Peter Hepplewhite (Hodder Wayland, 2005)

Websites

Find out about ships and life at sea at the National Maritime Museum website:
http://www.nmm.ac.uk/TudorExploration/NMMFLASH/

The Museum of London website has plenty of material to do with Tudor London, and how the city changed during Tudor times:
http://www.museumoflondon.org.uk/learning/features_facts/
    targettudors/index.html

This website has lots of fun facts about the Tudors, such as why sailors had to watch out for weevils in their food:
www.headlinehistory.co.uk

Places to visit

Visit the Tudor ship *Mary Rose*. The ship is now preserved in a museum after lying under the sea for more than 400 years.
Portsmouth Historic Dockyard
College Road, H M Naval Base
Portsmouth PO1 3LX
www.maryrose.org

Find out how a Tudor merchant's family would have lived and try on the clothes they would have worn.
Tudor Merchant's House
Quay Hill, Tenby SA70 7BX

Index